Terasa Gipson has earned a bachelor's in psychology, a master's in library science from the University of New York at Buffalo, and a Public Librarian's Professional Certificate from the University of the State of New York Education Department.

Ms. Gipson is a librarian and an adjunct professor at SUNY Buffalo State University.

She has been published in Library Journal, Family Circle, Buffalo News, ArtsWestchester Magazine, and ArtVoice. Moreover, she wrote a monthly online column for the International Institute of Buffalo – Refugee Resettlement Program highlighting host families.

She currently lives in Western New York with her husband.

In the Wake of Things is her first book.

In memory of my parents and the many other family members who have passed on. Your lives were a necessary part in the continuation of our family's existence.

Terasa Gipson

IN THE WAKE OF THINGS

AUSTIN MACAULEY PUBLISHERS™

LONDON • CAMBRIDGE • NEW YORK • SHARJAH

Ordering Information
Quantity sales: Special discounts are available on quantity purchases by corporations, associations, and others. For details, contact the publisher at the address below.

Publisher's Cataloging-in-Publication data
Gipson, Terasa
In the Wake of Things

ISBN 9781685625351 (Paperback)
ISBN 9781685625368 (ePub e-book)

Library of Congress Control Number: 2023905104

www.austinmacauley.com/us

First Published 2023
Austin Macauley Publishers LLC
40 Wall Street,33rd Floor, Suite 3302
New York, NY 10005
USA

mail-usa@austinmacauley.com
+1 (646) 5125767

To my Lord and Savior, Jesus – without Him, this book would not be a reality.

To Sister Mary Anna Falbo who realized my potential and encouraged me to become a writer.

To my husband, Mac – by reaching the top of your mountain, it has given me the courage to reach the top of mine.

To my sisters, Salina, Anita, and Marina, my first family. Our shared connection has bonded us throughout life. Your love and support have been a life-changer.

To my brothers, Trunnis II and David, although many years span between us, we are connected forever.

To my children, Darnell, Camille, Ian, and my grandchildren. You are my legacy. I will love you always.

To Nikki, my stepdaughter, much love, and respect. Continue to live your best life.

Ophelia Morey, thank you for the many years of friendship and inspiration.

Jennifer Campbell, I appreciate all the times you have encouraged me to read my poems with you at open mic nights. You have been my motivator and friend.

Finally, many thanks to all the people at Austin Macauley Publishers who have taken my manuscript from creation to publication. It is a dream come true.

Table of Contents

Part I
Legacy

Be mindful of the life you live, for all its worth will be
passed on after you,
whether good or not.

Days of Old

A rare moment arose
to ask my father about
those who lived before me.

I had longed to know
who they were
learn their stories
envision how their traits
matched my own.

I wondered if
a part of them
made its way
down to me
through flesh and blood.

At first, my inquiries
were met with hesitation
not certain if such a conversation
provoked unpleasant thoughts
best avoided
or
if the discussion needed a moment
to bring recollections into sharper view.
When he spoke

his words expressed
the essence of a people
whose strength and courage
carried on.

They did not give up.
They did not back away
from heartbreak and loss.
They endured hardships
to face another day.

Although,
descended from people
whose feet were set
in a country not their own,
exacted from them
everything one could possess
and made it possible
for the vision
of a new world
to be born
yet,
could not partake of its rewards.

Instead,
crowned their heads
with the belief and expectation
that one day
their bloodline
would receive the benefits
their lives were denied.

Midnight Star

Born in 1895.
Skin, the color of midnight.
Her eyes twinkled
like the evening stars.

A coat of iron
coursed through
the layers of her existence.

Segregation
and the mistreatment
of her people
was all she knew.

Straight-talking, tough
independent woman
earned her way
through the lock-jawed
grit of survival,
refusing to be extinct.

She raised four daughters.
Forbade them to marry men
within their race.
She believed a better chance

for future generations
would be gained
by those of a lighter persuasion.

She survived the loss
of two husbands.

Left to farm the land
of her inheritance,
she thrusted into the ground
all the weight she carried
to produce the sustenance needed
to cultivate a life
in a world
where her kind
was not welcomed.

A Gentle Soul

Grandpa,
a quiet, humble man.
Spectator of engagement.
He kept his thoughts
tucked away
in the creases of examination.

Simplicity,
his path to higher achievement.
Stabilized his life's journey
from reservation to residence
in white man's region.

He married a brown-skinned woman
from another race
and carved out a niche
in family tradition.

He sowed seeds of variety
throughout the landscape
of his family.

He carried on in his Native ways.
Savored his unique appetite
for rare delicacies.

Chocolate covered ants
were one of his favorite
evening snacks.

He kept one cheek
filled with tobacco,
a part of his everyday appearance
as the clothes he wore.

In his last days,
he reaped a plentiful harvest
of family love
nurtured throughout the years
in the rich soil
of his gentle kindness
bundled together
as a colorful bouquet
lasting a lifetime.

A Woman Denied

Stretched out long and wide
were dark days of light
for a child who was born
whose skin was not white.

She was born at a time
back in the day
when skin color ruled
and decided the way.

She was given a name
which meant strength and power.
Taught to surpass her limits
to go beyond being dour.

She was clothed in style
class and grace.
She never thought herself less
because of her race.

She grew up to believe
with hard work and dedication.
Her life would be better
no matter her education.

Blessed with the wisdom
to guide her decisions.
She possessed many traits
worthy of recognition.

Determined to live
each day of her life
pushing through hardships
struggles and strife.

Yet,
never given the chance
to prove all her worth
was denied her right to be
long before her birth.

Altar Call

A hush
fell over the sanctuary
as the music to "Wade in the Water"
softly filled the room.

On cue,
the choir began to sing.
Bodies swayed back and forth
like blades of grass
responding to a gentle breeze.

New Believers
waited their turn
to be dipped in the pool
of rebirth.

When done,
they stood at the altar
to be welcomed by the church.

Seated in the pews
a grandfather watched
as his granddaughter

stood with the group.
Her family by her side.
He contemplated going forward
to join them.

For many years
he attended the same church
with his wife.
Sat in the same seat
and heard a lifetime of sermons.

He resisted the urge
to walk forward
and claim what had been
on his heart.

On that day,
he let go to what
held him back.

He stood up.
Walked down the aisle
toward the altar.
His eyes laser fixed
not looking to the right
or the left.

Heads turned.
Jaws dropped.

Whispers passed
among the congregation.
Tears spilled from eyes
who knew his spiritual struggle.

A lifetime of prayers
answered.

Southern Woman

Grandmother,
a quiet, unassuming
southern woman.

Robust in stature.
Spoke few words.
Her skilled hands
were her voice.
They were never idle.
Calloused from hard work.

A homemaker.
She raised many children.
Grandmother to many more.

Frugal in her ways
to accommodate
the needs of her family.

Slivers of bar soap
became shampoo.
Ripped stockings
became knotted knee-highs
or potpourri caches.
Leftovers became

creative masterpieces
for the next day's dining pleasure.
Nothing left to waste.

Early Saturday mornings
were carved out for trips
to the farmer's market
eager to gain a shopper's edge
on fresh picks of the day.

Sundays
after church,
the family gathered
at her house for dinner
to enjoy the abundant feast
she prepared ahead of time.

Once inside,
a whiff of her cooking
rushed to the senses.

Mouths watered.
Noses dimpled.
Folks scampered
ready to devour
everything in sight
like locust in a farmer's field.
Baked macaroni and cheese.
Fried chicken.
Collard greens.
String beans.

Candied yams and cornbread
filled plates to the brim.

Cakes and pies
made to order
decorated Grandma's buffet table
for family to take home to enjoy.

Everyone found a place
in the house
or in the yard
to relish her treats.

Tables and chairs
were strategically placed
in various spots around
the outdoor oasis
she designed.

Tall weeping willows
weighed down
thick with leaves
bent toward the ground.
A canopy for those
who sat under them.

Fruit trees and berry bushes
produced a colorful backdrop
for the many vegetable beds
dispersed throughout the wide spaces.
At the edge

of her garden
sat two white latticed trellises
covered with crawling red roses.

Parked beneath
the flowered awnings
sat picnic tables
which provided a favorite
shaded escape
from all the chaos
Sunday family dinners created.

Grandmother's love
permeated all
she touched.

She created beauty
from the dust
of a prudent life.

Now gone,
her spirit embodies
all she loved
no matter where
on Earth they may be.

Southern Man

Grandfather,
stifled by the Jim Crow South
decided to head north
with the hope
for a better life.

He left his family for a time
to secure a job and a home
for them.

Once achieved,
he sent for his family
to join him.

He landed work in a foundry.
Lived in a one-room shanty
on its premises
for months on end
focused on his goal.

The work, extremely difficult.
The heat, brutal.
The hours, long.
The machinery, dangerous.
Racial discrimination, rampant.

The foundry drained the life
from its workers.

Sheer determination
steadied his feet to the floor.
His mind rooted
toward a greater vision.

He regarded it
a rite of passage
earned by unwavering resolve.

He took hold of the American dream
mixed with the ironed blood
of his ancestors
and built a new path
for his offspring to tread
staking their place
in the land of opportunity.

Forever.

The Interventionist

Colorful
Interactive
Eccentric
were terms used
to describe the family matriarch.

Bold
fearless
full of energy
She refused to live
her life unnoticed.

She thrived on helping others
though her methods unconventional.

Spending time with her
as a child
was an adventure
into the unexpected.

Often,
during shopping trips
extensive conversations

were had with strangers.
Backward steps
quick glances at their watches
were the only ways to escape.

If someone presented
a physical challenge
or other signs of distress
she stopped them
found out about their condition
and offered unsolicited medical advice.

Sometimes,
her advice was followed
by a live demonstration
to ensure their understanding.

Most people
stood and watched
with patience and
polite smiles
as she illustrated an exercise routine
to alleviate pain or correct a disposition
like a yogi
in a yoga studio
working with a student.
Oblivious to watchful eyes around her.

Any grandchild who
accompanied her
during those moments
stood in silence
embarrassed by her theatrics.

When all was
said and done
a sigh of relief
was let out into the air.

Until,
once again,
her eyes became fixed
on another poor soul
and an intervention
would begin anew.

Passing On

Although they are gone,
their essence remains within.
Forever with us.

Part II
Heir

The recipient of an inheritance. One can choose to enrich it or impoverish it.

Fathers

Chosen to be
natural protectors
providers of the species
pillars of strength and courage.

Many will rise
and have risen
to a challenges
this role entails
recognizing success is in the trying.
Doing nothing is not an option.

Maturity affords them
the wisdom of knowing
their purpose is of great importance
too significant to dismiss.

Yet,
not every father
who has planted his seed
will reap the benefits
of his fruit.
With eyes wide open
he decides to take another path
blinded to the consequences

that lie ahead.
Unaware of the thorns
that will prick at his flesh
tearing open the raw substance
contained within.

To bind the wound
of this affliction
is to open the heart of acceptance.

So that
at any time
on any given day
forgiveness will meet reconciliation.

Self-Made in the USA

He grew up
in extreme poverty.

Enveloped with the
shame of lack
like garments
strapped tight to his being.

Parents with
more mouths to feed
and bodies to clothe
than skill and ability
could provide.

The little boy
tucked himself
into a small room
and made a promise.

He vowed that
in the years ahead
poverty would not
cling to his destiny.
He would accomplish
unimaginable dreams.

Break through a life
of hardship and want
to join the residents
of another community.
Those not shackled
by society's restraints.

Nine years old
marked the beginning
of a lifetime commitment
toward his goal.

With a red flyer wagon
as his companion
he offered curbside delivery service
to seniors who walked
to the neighborhood market
and needed help
bringing their groceries home.

He carried a shoeshine kit
in his wagon.
Shined shoes for businessmen
who wanted a crisp look
from head to toe.

When he became a man,
he traded his wagon
for factory work.

On weekends,
changed tires
at an auto shop.

Used his saved earnings
to purchase a truck
and delivered goods across the country.

One truck became two
and then three.

When the economy changed
he sold his trucks
repurposed his financial gain
into another business
more profitable than the last.

One undertaking
after another.
He earned more.
Invested more.
Expanded more.

Lived the life
he dreamed of living.
No holds barred.
No time in his life
for those he brought into it.
Too busy turning obstacles
into stepping-stones.

Yet,
toward the end of his life
he looked back
to view the road
he had traveled
only to realize
his dream costed him everything.

The Hawk

The Hawk was
a shrewd businessman.
Wheeler and dealer of propositions
that favored his highest objective.

Held on tight to his money
as he reached for more.

Owned real estate
among other enterprises.
Kept a close eye
on his currency.

Collected his money from tenants
with the skill of a hawk
lasered in on its prey.

He created unique ways
to seize his rent
from those who tried
to escape their monthly commitment
for more pleasurable pastimes.
He learned their habits.
Knew where his tenants worked.
Scoped out their nighttime hangouts

or favorite watering holes.
Collected addresses and phone numbers
of significant others.
He left nothing to chance.

All account information
was stored in his head
like a photograph.
Details recited when needed
as if from a ledger book.

He would stake out
in his car for hours.
Hid around street corners.
Approached his tenants
before they entered
their destinations.
He drove them to the bank
or check cashing establishments
if necessary.

He took payment
whether partial or in full.

There was no shame
in his game.
His purpose was to
collect what was due him
before it vanished like mist.
By day's end
his mind was not yet at rest

because he believed
there was no peace
for the weary
and no room for the broke.

Home Training

Father
was a student of the streets.
Lived by his carnal instincts.
Trial and error, his education.

Rebelled against
the Bible teachings
of his youth.

Thought he knew
a better way.

When his daughters
became teenagers,
he felt it prudent
to impart his insights
to them.

Roundtable sessions
were commonplace
during mealtime.

Such lessons
were greeted
with polite impatience.

Sideways glances.
Twitchy fingers
that drum rolled
under the table.
Legs fidgeted about nervously
waiting for the moment
to bolt.

Speaking on matters
meant for a future time.
Conversations too grown up
for adolescent minds
who were not ready to care about such things.

Their sights were set on immediate concerns.
Calling friends.
Making plans.
Hanging out.
Cute boys.
The latest high school gossip.

"Pay Attention!" rang out
when their distracted minds
seemed obvious.

And then,
one day
during dinner,
he said,

"When you are older
and challenges arise,
remember my teachings
so you will be wise.

Like the morning light
after the night has passed,
my words will guide you.
It is wisdom that will last.

In difficult moments
when darkness hovers long,
remember our conversations
and keep on going strong.

It is the only real gift
I have to give to you
and one day
you will look back
and know that to be true."

Mister

Saddened by the loss of his wife
a man had bought a parrot.
He hoped it would relieve the pain
as he tried hard to bear it.

His green-feathered companion
became a true and faithful friend.
His days were much brighter
as his darkness began to descend.

The man named the parrot Mister
because the bird heeded his voice.
When the man came home from work
his feathered friend rejoiced.

While rooted on his shoulder
he taught his friend new tricks.
Together they cooked in the kitchen
then later watched action flicks.

When no one was at home
Mister soared throughout the house.
He never made a mess.
He was quiet as a mouse.

Mister was also a fast learner.
He mimicked new words each day.
Every night before his bedtime
repeated his master's words to pray.

One evening when the man came home
he found Mister lying still in his cage.
The man mourned the loss of his friend
because his sadness had been assuaged.

Heart of the Matter

A father
spent his days
at his kitchen table
looking out of the window
weary and alone.

His eyes transfixed
to an unknown place
beyond the outer view.

Flashes of haunting memories
darted before him.
Decayed images obscured his vision.
Bodies of the disenfranchised
littered the wake
of his unspoken life.

Scarred souls tossed about
like spewed debris
along the path of his discontent.

Hardened by the choices
he ruthlessly made.
Felt justified in his prideful ways.

Restlessness choked his days.
Sleep escaped his nights.
Isolated from those
who could restore his soul.

Healing was not an option
for his unrepentant life.

But,
stricken one morning
in a fleeting moment.
Brought on by the angst of his past.

He moved to survey a room
filled with his forgotten memories
tucked away like forbidden secrets.

Among his possessions
he found a pair of roller skates
that belonged to
the wife of his youth.

A vision appeared in his mind.
The sight of a beautiful woman
dressed in cuffed blue jeans.

Her thick raven hair
was pulled back behind her ears.
A long braid twisted like rope

and tied in a knot
glimmered in the radiance
of her beauty.

Silver-hooped earrings
dangled from her ears
reflected the evening light
as in a mirror.
She had slipped
into his heart
as soft as a whisper
and penetrated
the depth of his resistance.
The memory of her
flooded his barren soul.

And then,
in a breath
the vision was gone
like the morning dew
erased at the hint of sunlight.

With her essence still lingering
in the space of his emptiness
he cuddled the skates
against his bosom
and tried not to succumb
to a force unnatural to him.
Prompted by the memory
he decided to send the skates
to the daughter of her likeness.

The receipt of this gift
uplifted her soul.
Gratitude filled her heart.

Satisfied
with this kind act,
the man returned
to the kitchen table
and looked out of the window
hopeful.

Eyes of Silence

For a dying father
the moment was near.

Hazy visions pressed into
the tiny spaces
where life still existed.

No time left
to claim what was lost
to give back what was taken
to make right all the wrongs.

He could not say
what needed to be said
to those who needed to hear it.

He could not be expected
to be like others.
To give what he did not possess
within him.

Now,
as the shadow of death
loomed over him
ready to take all that still lingered

unspoken sorrows
consumed all the light
that remained
from the windows of his soul
closing them forever.

In the Wake of Things

The time had come
to lay to rest
a man admired by many
but known by few.

A powerhouse of strength
thought to be immortal
but now, his threshold had ended.

His family arrived
before the appointed time.
Allowed a private moment
for prayers and final goodbyes.

A finely dressed man
waited near the entrance
of the Chapel for the Rested
ready to escort the way.

The parlor was cool
brisk like the morning air.
Floral impressions
sprinkled the walls
designed to bring comfort
to its guests.

Nestled against the back panel
sat a silver-and-chrome casket
laced with white roses
and baby's breath.
The Mercedes of burial motif.

The best in death
as lived in life
for a man who
accepted nothing less.

I stood
over the familiar stranger
lying peacefully
in his white satin bed.

Words could not express
the barren weight from within.

Those who were like precious gems
got lost in a mound
of more important things.

Thus,
as the years passed,
the gap grew wider
the emptiness deepened
and forged ahead

like the river waters
flowing down stream
never to break
the surface again.

Part III
Heiress

Entitled to the legacy of a predecessor.
Wisdom will increase the legacy's blessings. The lack of it
will destroy its intentions.

Mothers

Chosen to be
life-bearers
caregivers
soul-molders
made from the
loving hands of God.

Rich as earthly soil.
Seeds of the future
planted within her.
Equipped to fulfill her purpose.

Though,
not every mother
is able to sustain
her birthright.

So,
others rise
to take her place.
To nurture one
from the bounty

of their riches
to completion.

Sugar and Spice

She was twelve years old.
Wore two thick ponytails
draped in the front
past her shoulders.
The ends tied with pink ribbons.

Her eyes sparkled like fairy dust
against the radiance of her
smooth cocoa-colored skin.
A playful smile highlighted
her sunny disposition.

Her parents had little money,
but among the few things she owned
was a pearl necklace
left to her by her grandmother.
It was the young girl's
most prized possession.

She wore the necklace every day.
with the hope that one day
she would fall in love

with a rich man
have a family
live in a beautiful home
and own lots of nice things.

A dream set in her heart
learned from storybook tales
about princesses who were swept away
by knights in shining armors
who lived in castles far away.
They would love each other
and live happily ever after.
The end.

And then,
she grew up.

Double Date

Two sisters,
prepped for a night out
with two boys
they met at school.

An evening
of outdoor skating
to the sounds of bee-bop
and swing music
a popular pastime
for teens back in the day.

Their male companions
showed off
their fancy skate moves
to the amazement of the crowd.

Their risky maneuvers
threatened to earn them
a trip to the hospital
outfitted with the latest cast wear.
Anything to impress the ladies.
Adolescent notions
of marriage and babies
danced around in their heads

choreographed to the skate music
playing in the background.
They believed to have found
the answer to their dreams.

Naïve to the way of life and love
and the uncertain terrain ahead.

Prelude to Desire

A gray haze
enveloped the view
outside her apartment window.

Tiny feather-like crystals
gently fell to the ground.

Bare treetops bowed
to the heavy winds
whipping up layers of white dust
from the places it had settled.

Demands of the
morning tasks
created anticipation for
an afternoon prelude
with a young man
recently introduced to her
through a mutual friend.

Out of the window
she spotted the baby blue T-Bird
he drove.
The soft sound of chimes
indicated her date had arrived.

A quick glance
through the door's peephole
revealed a dark shadowy figure
standing in the hallway.

Dressed in Italian leather
from shoulder to shoes
the young man stood
waiting for an invitation
to enter.

She opened the door
and waved him in.
As he passed by her
the provocative scent of British sterling
trailed behind him.
A shiver of desire
shimmied through her inner parts.

Greetings were exchanged.
Expectations dispelled.

His charm radiated
through the confident way
he spoke.
Conditions outside
went unnoticed.

Intense winds
pushed through the air
and battered the windowpanes.

The opaque vision of
white mass
captured their attention.

Trapped inside
by the power unleashed
in an unusual winter storm.

Both seized the chance
to become more familiar
over the next three days.

Veiled

The Maid-of-Honor
drew the veil
over the face
of the bride to be.

It was the finishing touch
before the walk down
the church aisle
to marry a man
the bride barely knew.

On the eve
before the wedding
a revelation came
for her not to go forth
with the ceremony.

Unwilling to back away
from what she believed
was her promised hope
she pulled the veil
over her eyes

and walked toward
the turbulent years
of a life she could not have imagined
and remained within its walls
till death do her part.

Our Mother

In my mind's eye
I see a vision
of a beautiful woman
with smooth chocolate
colored skin.

It reminds me
of the sweet
scent of Chanel
that accompanied her hugs.

She wears
a conservative smile
upon her face
as though thoughtfully
weighing her kindnesses
to be revealed.

A woman
who in her day
left the house
complete with hat and gloves.

A woman
who taught her daughters
to sit up straight
and cross their legs.

To always
look their best
and not act silly
around boys
or we would never
snag husbands
when we grew up.

She wanted us
to be ladies
just like her.

Now gone
without the chance
to see her daughters
become the ladies
she taught us to be.

Just like her.

Working with Wood

Hindsight,
always the great clarifier
when truth is overruled by desire
the unsteady, rocky blast of new love.

Lingered looks from star-kissed eyes
set deep in the wells of promise.
His tender hands caressed
the nape of her neck.

Sensual words whispered
from soft wet lips
trickled down to
the depths of her core.
Desire's grip clung tight
to her senses.

Passion grew
until the two lives
merged like hybrids
transformed into something new.

Now,
awakened by the reality
of an invisible force
instinct revealed
that something had changed.

Doubt rushed in
like a thousand raindrops.
Quick, short breaths
tried to push away the lies
that coursed through her
of a love that never was.

The scent of betrayal
permeated her sense of being.
Lying lips pressed against her mouth.
Her heart became like wood
hardened to his deceptive ways.

Deaf to the urgency of repair.
Stained from the loss
of what she believed to be true.
Now gone.

Secrets in the Bedroom

Her bedroom
strictly off limits.
It was a private space
to her personal world.

The allure of it
much too tempting
to ignore.

Once over the threshold
into her room
one was immersed
in the sights and scents
of femininity.

Inhaling the fragrance
of a blooming garden
bursting in shades of pink.

Rose-colored shears
hung loosely at the windows
which encased the outer view
like a framed landscape.
Underneath the window
sat a long bench seat

decorated with soft feathery pillows
in floral design
that occupied the space
against the wall.

A pink chinchilla bedspread
blanketed the mahogany bed.
An open armoire near her bed
showcased dressy hats
made with fancy lace,
tulle, beads, and rhinestones
worn on special occasions
especially to Sunday morning church services.

Situated on her dresser
lay a gold-trimmed
mirrored accessory tray
with matching comb and hairbrush
reminiscent of a foregone era.

Beautifully diamond cut
glass perfume bottles
attached with spray pumps
sat atop her vanity.
Each filled with floral scents.

An array of nail polishes
and make-up
arranged on lace doilies
and placed on both sides of the tray.

In the corner
next to the dresser
stood a tall mahogany jewelry box.

Hanging from its hooks
draped pearl and diamond
necklaces and gold bracelets.

Tucked away in the lower part
of the jewelry box
contained sparkling gold rings
earrings, broaches, and pins.

Her dresser drawers
revealed carefully folded
lace underwear
colorful scarves
delicate shear stockings
wrapped neatly in tissue paper
as protection against wood splinters.

Her closet,
an eclectic assortment
of expensive clothing.

Each garment graced with
satin-covered hangers
topped with a satin bow.

Shoe racks dangled
from the closet door
which displayed the latest
footwear for every occasion.

A boudoir fit for a queen.

But…

the bedroom
held secrets
that told a different story.

Upon a closer look,
hidden in dresser drawers
underneath beautifully folded
lace and satin
one would find
white-capped containers
filled with remedies
to relieve a broken heart.

Hidden in the back of the closet
behind her expensive clothes
a stack of flowered hat boxes

packed with more promises
assured to soften the blows
of harsh realities
on a weakened soul.
Under her soft feathery pillows

lie the explicit night reading
of a love-starved woman
seeking pleasure within its pages.

So,
each night
she retreated to her bedroom
surrounded by its alluring charm
and exquisite beauty
into a haven of her own creation.

Lost and Found

The fire raged
on the second floor
of our family's two-story home.

Flickered fingers
of heated anger
reached out to grasp
everything within its reach.

It lapped up roof tiles
and shingles
like melted cotton candy.

People crowded corners
to watch our house
burn bright
against the midnight sky.

Sighs of astonishment grew
among the herd of people
attracted by the fiery light.

I stood paralyzed
among the crowd
praying that

whatever truly mattered
would not be lost
but be kept safe.

Many years later,
a detour took me back
to the place where
our family once lived.

To my surprise,
I arrived as the house
was being demolished.
Debris was scattered everywhere.

An unexpected sight
to witness.
Our childhood home
being dismantled
after so many years.
Destine to become
a grassy knoll.

I contemplated
my presence here
at that moment.

Was it by chance
I happened upon this place
that many years before
brought such sadness?

Or,
was the detour divinely ordered
as an answer to a long-ago prayer
to let me know
that everything that truly mattered
still remained?

Burned Twice

A young girl returned
home from school.

As she entered the house,
she heard the silky voice
of Peter Nero playing
softly on the stereo
wafting through the house.

It signaled that her mother
was in good spirits.

The girl walked down
the long narrow hallway
that led to her mother's bedroom.
She halted at the doorway.

The vision of her mother
as she sat at her vanity table
eyes transfixed on her mirrored reflection
aroused curiosity and fear
within the young girl.

She watched, unnoticed
as her mother stroked
the puckered skin
grafted on her forehead.

Her gaze shifted to her hands
awkwardly positioned
on the vanity tabletop.

Hands robbed
of their former beauty.
Fingers she no longer recognized.
Her long stems remained
stiff and rigid,
a web of fleshy colored skin
wrapped around them.

Her sorrow visible
from behind hollow eyes.
Once, full of hope
with dreams that kissed the stars
now, lived caught
in the crosshairs
between despair and hope.

Her daughter
attuned to the wounds
of her mother's past
realized the cost

of her sacrifice.
Her loss
far outweighed her gain
bound to an eternal broken heart.

Suddenly,
aware of her daughter's presence
her mother offered a slight smile.

She revealed that
a long-ago friend
invited her out again
for dinner and dancing.

Before her mother's tragic accident
she often went out
with her male companion.

Excited for her mother,
the girl moved closer
to her side.

She watched
as her mother struggled
to apply her make-up.
Stringent fingers strained
to conceal her scars.

The promise of
a rekindled relationship
gave her mother
the courage to look her best.

Already dressed
in an elegant evening gown
she added the final touches
to her face.

She swiped red lipstick
across her lips,
then pressed them
into a soft tissue
to dab away the excess.

A mist of Chanel No. 5
was applied to her neck
and a pat behind her ears.

Her daughter walked
over to the living room window
and watched for the friend to arrive.

Her mother
sat perched on the edge
of the couch
and lightly smoothed out
the folds of her
black evening gown.
She waited.

A headdress of
clustered curls
piled high atop the crown
of her head
exposed cultured pearl earrings
matched with a pearl necklace
draped around her neck.

She waited.

A few strands of her hair
fell loose
from her neatly
side-swiped bang.
She tucked the strands
behind her ears.

She waited.

Nervous fingers
clutched her necklace.
Uncertainty pressed in.

She waited.

The sound of bell chimes
never came.

The promise of new love
dashed before its reality.
Slowly,
her mother rose
from the couch.

The daughter
followed her mother
into the bedroom
and helped her undress.

The gown was returned
to its satin hanger.
Slipped back
into the recesses of her closet
where it will spend
the rest of its days
unworn.

And,
like her evening gown
her mother receded to a dark place
where she spent
the rest of her days
alone.

Thief in the Night

It was evening.

The tiny kitchen
was wrapped in family laughter
stemming from a trash-talking
games of cards.

The sweet aroma
of fried chicken
and baked biscuits
saturated the air around us.

Down the hallway
in another room
a frantic voice
surged through
the clamor in the kitchen.

The sound grew
more intense
with every step
toward its direction.

Seated uncomfortably
at the edge of the bed
sat my mother with
desperation in her eyes.

An urgent plea
to call for help
emerged from her lips.

A swift glance
at her appearance
seemed not to warrant
such an emergency.

Concern crossed my face.
Hesitation pulled me backward.
Her narrowed eyes
flashed like darts
signaled that I do
as I was told.

My fingers quickened
to her command.

The paramedics arrived.

Family rushed from the kitchen
scared and confused.
Reassurances were given
to defuse further drama.

The medics ushered her
from the house
to the ambulance.

Before reaching it
her body slumped over.
She was carried
the rest of the way.

They hoisted her
into the rear of the vehicle.
I hopped onto the passenger seat.

Doors slammed.
Sirens screamed.
Flashes of fragmented scenes
streaked past the window.

Behind me
hurried motions
and muffled voices
worked to penetrate my fears.

Tears pooled
at the rims of my eyelids.
The salty liquid
refused to tumble over.

My façade of strength
threatened to come undone.
Near the hospital entrance,

awaited medical staff
equipped with life-saving gear
to resurrect the woman
who was quickly slipping away.
Inside,
I waited.
Afraid to breathe.
Nervous for what was to come.

Bright lights
Eerie sounds
of quiet stillness
emanated from the hospital corridor.

I sat with eyes closed.
Forced myself to draw breath.

I did not see the doctor
who waited patiently before me.
His soft, gentle voice
confirmed my suspicion.

His words
hung in the air
like a cloud of thick smoke
crowding the space
around me.

The layers
beneath my skin
burned with sorrow.

Distraught by the pain
of death and abandonment.
Not yet able
to fully grasp
the weight of the situation

but knew
that one day this moment would come.
It was always implied.
The notion surrounded me
like a forgone conclusion.

The allure
of multi-colored beauties
captured her attention
many years ago.
They came with the promise
of easing the pain.

An insatiable craving
that demanded more and more
slowly extracted the state
of her existence.

Until,
their slick deceitful lies
silenced her forever
robbing her of life
like a thief in the night.

Litany of Confession

Do not be mad
because I chose
a way to peace
and not be sad.

Do not be angry
because I chose
to face the end
with my dignity.

Do not be discouraged
because I chose
to walk my final steps
with grace and courage.

Do not be upset
because I chose
to embrace my last moments
without regrets.

Do not be downhearted
because I chose
to keep silent my pain
before I departed.

So, if you can
forgive my choice
celebrate my life
like the day it began.

Buried Treasure

A black limousine
rolled slowly through
the stone-pillared entrance.

It veered along
the narrow snow-plowed road
passing tombstones
which framed both sides
of the pathway.

Names deeply
etched in marble
of those who had
gone before.

Their places reserved
in the bosom of the earth
forever.

Ahead,
a vision emerged.

Four cloth covered chairs
positioned in perfect symmetry
faced the direction
of the final resting place.

Teenage women
dressed in black
emerged from the limousine.

They led the way forward.
The crowd followed behind
and formed a half circle
around them.

Hands pressed down
on their shoulders
for comfort and support.

Quiet whispers of prayers
interrupted the silence.

A man
dressed in black
stood before the gathered.

He opened a small brown book
and cupped it in his gloved hands.

A flurry of words
passed through his lips
into the dry icy air.
Scriptures read
but not heard.

Grief held captive
the attention of those
who came to pay their respects.

A treasured woman
who gave all she had
until she was no more.

Grave Findings

Trudging through the soggy grass
mud wrapped around my shoes.
Anxious to reach the place
where solace is most true.

I hurried past a row of graves
until I reached the spot.
Expected to see my mother's name
but instead saw an empty plot.

The earth around her marker
severely out of place.
The stone with her engravings
was not in its proper space.

Tossed far from its location
way across the field.
Shattered in a million pieces.
Rendered my steps stilled.

A gaping hole exposed
a dark abyss below.
A mangled mix of grass and gravel
ejected with a blow.

Uncertain of what this meant.
No reasonable answer could fathom.
My mind gave way to strange illusions
which came and went at random.

I imagined my mother's spirit
rose from her place of rest.
Prompted by a desperate plea
from someone who knew me best.

I heard a faint whisper
on the edge of the wind.
A reassurance that she is not far away
just remember to look within.

Part IV
Progeny

Legacy bearers – where the seeds of hope from those
before
germinate new possibilities.

Sisterhood

Sisters,
born into the world
each with their unique splendor.
Given gifts from above
only time will render.

Decorated in shades
of caramel, honey, chocolate, and brown.
Loving, fighting, teasing and
Laughing all abound.

Each one very different
and yet they are the same.
Sharing ancestral lineage
together as their claim.

When we listen closely
we will clearly hear
gathered wisdom whispered
softly in our ears.

From each other's struggles
presents life's many tests.
Once lessons are learned
Can be passed on to the rest.

It is such a comfort
if in the end we find
the true meaning of sisters
are hearts that are aligned.

In the Middle

Couched between siblings
anxious to rise above the fray
to make her presence known
each and every day.

She took charge at playtime.
Skilled at achieving her way.
Maneuvered situations to her favor
no matter what others had to say.

The young girl's confident ability
would someday serve her well.
Embodied with determination of purpose
a quality needed to excel.

The Observer

Sister number three
lived under the radar.
She had the ability
to be gifted by far.

Not the first one born
no significant model to set.
Shielded from parental scorn
if expectations were not met.

Her quiet stealth like motions
away from watchful eyes
gave way to observe the notions
older siblings usually devised.

She knew not everything
had to be experienced firsthand
others helped smooth out the terrain
which gave her a place to land.

Not to be mistaken
as one who is unknown
her presence not forsaken
the future was much her own.

Last

A child born last
has its unique charm.
Their arrival can bring much excitement
or spark as much alarm.

The youngest in the family
sets them up to gain
the wisdom and experience
years of parenting have sustained.

Although many times,
older siblings play parent roles
the youngest learn to find their way
when given room to grow.

Their position is just as important
as the ones who came before
because they complete the family story
for there will be no more.

Our Kitchen

The knotty pine walls of our kitchen
encased many years of
table-side conversations
and family connections.

It was where
we listened to
Motown music on the radio
during mealtime.

It was where
girlhood discussions took place
that we thought
were of the utmost priority.

It was where
beginner cooking lessons
were exercised
which consisted of burnt food
and undercooked meat.

It was where
we learned how to press and curl
our thick, coarse hair at the stove
using a hot comb and curling iron

long before the invention
of electric hair tools.

Consequently,
it was where
many tears were shed
from burnt scalps, hair loss
and other styling mishaps
which occurred while we mastered
the skill of self-grooming.

It was where
our dog Sandy
spent most of his time
eating the unwanted food
that fell to the floor
on purpose from the kitchen table.

It was where
my dad sat down with me
at eleven years old
to have the awkward conversation
about what he called
the "birds and the bees."

He told me
to keep my dress down
and my legs closed.
That brief chat
left me bewildered
and uncomfortable.

Naïve to what he meant
but afraid to ask,
I wondered what
wildlife and insects
had to do with anything.

I thought, "Who walked around
with their dress up?
How would I be able to walk
if my legs were closed?"

Eventually,
I figured it out.

Our kitchen
was the best place
in the house to be.

It was where
family remained
the most important
ingredient on the menu.

Third Floor Sanctuary

Wire mesh covered
the small windows
in our attic playroom.

The mesh served as a safeguard
designed to keep curious little girls
from venturing out
beyond their boundaries.

The walls were blanketed with
a bouquet of pink flowered wallpaper
painted on a dark gray backdrop.

There were wooden toy boxes
stuffed to the rim.
Plenty of choices
that kept little minds
and hands busy.

A two-story dollhouse
complete with miniature furniture
and a little family.
Role play for the future.

Barbie dolls equipped with clothes,
shoes and accessories.
Each doll had its own carrying case.
Useful for pretend sleepovers and family trips.

Two desks, a chalkboard, and an easel
offered opportunities for creativity.
Pretending to be a teacher was the favorite.
No one wanted to be the student,
so we reluctantly took turns.

A Fisher-Price kitchen,
a table and chair set,
and an easy-bake oven
used to entertain imaginary friends
who stopped by for
occasional visits
after our dolls went to bed.

After dinner,
tea was served
from the China tea set
given to us as a gift
from a relative
who lived very far away,
maybe even in China!

Our attic playroom
was the sanctuary for our
limitless and ever-changing imaginations.
It was a place for pretend
and discovery.

A place where we were
free to be ourselves,
before innocence unfastened
and adult life changed everything.

Sweet Sublime

Life in a child's mind
is a world of wonder
and discovery.

Their imagination takes
incredible journeys
into the realm of impossibilities.

Watching favorite cartoons
with the belief that
what was happening on
the television screen
was real life.

Like Mr. Magoo
who drove around in his car
completely blind.
Banged into everything, unscathed
and lived to do it again
another day.

Like Tom and Jerry
who survived more broom thrashings
beating the odds of sudden death

and proved the point
that cats have nine lives
maybe more.

How about the many miles
Wiley Coyote covered
chasing after the Road Runner?
He was always outwitted.
He never caught the fastest creature alive.

What about Fred Flintstone
and Barney Rubble.
Their makeshift transportation
put together with logs
stones and animal skins.

Their bottomless car
held up with their hands
propelled by foot power.

They never stubbed their toes
suffered skin burns
or built muscle mass.

I guess that was why
they racked up such a huge
appetite for Din-o-ribs
T-Rex T-Bone steaks
and Dinosaur eggs.

The Swim Lesson

One summer weekend
our dad decided to take
his four daughters
to the campground he owned
miles from the city.

He needed to check on the campers
and do some repairs
on a few of the cabins.
We played while he worked.

Later
when he was done,
he decided to teach us how to swim
in the quarry located in the middle
of the campground.

To him,
we were getting older
and needed to learn this skill
before the fear of water
set in.
Scared,

but willing to learn
life jackets were strapped
on us over our clothes.

Next,
we were hoisted into the air
one by one
and tossed into the quarry.

Loud screams
rushed along the airwaves
causing ripples of fear
for the onlookers.

We landed in the water
like rocket missiles.

Once stabilized
on the surface of the water,
we bobbed up and down
like four buoys
marking the place
where we landed.

Terrified to move,
we tried to stay
as still as possible
not wanting to sink
or arouse the creatures
that swam below.

Eventually,
we were scooped
out of the water
like dead fish
floating along the surface.

Our swim lesson
was not as successful
as our dad thought it would be.

To this day,
his daughters are not swimmers.

Not certain
if that experience
stunted the will
to learn how to swim.

But,
as for me,
I am certain of this:
water is beautiful and powerful
to be admired and respected
from the shore.

Summer Camp

Every summer
we were sent to camp
for two weeks of fun
to romp and tramp.

A wooded haven
with plenty of space.
Perfect for learning
new things to embrace.

Activities created
to stimulate mind, body, and soul.
Like hiking, swimming, canoeing
or play acting a role.

At night in the dorms
before the lights went out
tales of ghost stories
were passed all about.

Sleepy children
too scared to sleep.
Stayed awake all night
without making a peep.

When camp was over
it was hard to believe.
The time had come
for everyone to leave.

Saying goodbye
to friends we had made.
Hoping to see them again
before memories of them fade.

Glad to go home
to share what we learned.
Looked forward to next summer
when we would return.

World's Fair

We took a family trip
to Expo 67 World's Fair.
Held in Montreal, Quebec, Canada
We could not wait to get there.

There were millions of people
traipsing all around.
Our little feet hardly kept up
without falling down.

Our eyes feasted on all
the odd shapes and multi-colors.
Of people from every nation
who represented many cultures.

Man and His World
was the theme of the year.
Each pavilion showcased
how people lived in their sphere.

Man as explorer, worker
artist and provider.
Living in community
to make things much brighter.

Our parents were excited
to see all the exhibits.
We wandered from one to the other
getting bored by the minute.

My sisters and I
were too young to understand or care.
Just wanted to go to children's world
and ride the rides at the World's Fair.

Christmas Past and Present

In the early evening
our neighborhood and all around
Christmas lights shine from every house
adorning the dark streets in town.

Block after block
windows displayed
Christmas trees of all sizes
fully dressed in holiday array.
Beautifully wrapped surprises
sit under each Christmas tree.
Waiting for the proper time
to open them with glee.

Christmas Eve night
is the only time of year
when children willingly go to bed early
for Santa to appear.

Little eyes grow weary
too tired to hear
Santa bringing gifts and toys
on his sled with his reindeer.

Eggnog and cookies
left out for a treat
for Santa and his helpers
ready to eat.

In the early morning hours,
excited children arise
to see if what they wished for
was under the tree by surprise.

Sounds of gladness and joy
rang throughout each house.
Arousing moms and dads from their sleep
to check out all the shouts.

While high above beyond the sky
louder than the noise on earth.
A chorus of angels raise their voice
to sing praise for Christ's birth.

To those who know the story
that is behind the season.
Give honor to the greatest gift of all
for Jesus is the reason.

Visits with Santa

Christmas season downtown
dazzled with lots of light.
Wreaths and candy cane garland
sparkled in the night.

Department store windows
showcased magical themes.
Tin soldiers and toy trains
made from little children's dreams.

Beautiful nativity scenes
outfitted in all its array.
Depicting Joseph, Mary, and baby Jesus
on his birthday.

Red velvet ropes
draped on golden poles.
Stretched across sidewalks
to navigate traffic flow.

Inside department stores
elves were busy at work.
Greeting all the customers
and helping the store clerks.

They gathered all the gifts
to load on Santa's sleigh.
Checking for the name tags
to deliver them on Christmas day.

Little ones so delighted
for just a moment with Santa.
They asked for permission to see him
from their moms or their nannas.

They stand in a line
waiting to be seated on the throne
just for a chance to speak directly
to Santa Claus alone.

Once on his lap
they are not shy to say
what they hope to see
under the tree on Christmas day.

Easter

A time when
little boys wore suits
little girls wore fancy dresses
donned patent leather shoes
and socks with ruffled edges.

Hats and gloves
fit for the occasion
ready to go to church
to show appreciation.

Weeks before Easter
each child is given
a scripture to memorize
about Christ who has risen.

On Easter Sunday
they stood before the church.
All eyes were held captive
as each read their memory verse.

Some children were confident
to deliver their lines.
Others were afraid to speak
and began to whine.

When the program was over
the children were relieved.
The audience applauded proudly
at what they had achieved.

Innocence Preserved

When I grew up
back in the day,
adults gathered together
children were made to go play.

Their mature conversations
were not meant for children's ears.
Matters too grown up
for younger ones to hear.

They believed children
should be with those their own age.
Not allowed to linger around
to listen to adults engage.

Natural curiosities
made our antennas rise high.
Because we had been excluded
we tried to find out why.

One child would hang back
pretending to tie their shoe.
Another one walked away slowly
before a stern voice shouted, "You too!"

We were always surprised
when caught at our childish tricks.
Clueless that adults were once young
and could share some of their tips.

But,
my mother and grandmother
had a trick of their own.
When children came around
they spoke Pig Latin alone.

Since their conversation
could not be understood
Playing amongst ourselves
seemed to be pretty good.

Saturdays at Auntie's House

Every Saturday morning
we woke up to the smell
of the lemony scent of sweetness
that we knew oh so well.

The aroma waffled through our noses
getting us out of bed
with hunger pangs in our bellies
and thoughts of sweet tastes in our heads.

A warm, golden pound cake
would be lifted from the oven.
Joined with hot dogs and pork-n-beans
to share with our cousins.

Saturday potlucks
at my auntie's house
was a day spent with family
for everyone gathered about.

The smaller children played
while the teens talked and danced.
The women were busy in the kitchen.
And the men played games of chance.

Everybody feasted on
the smorgasbord of food and fun.
Soon, it would be time to leave
when all was said and done.

Exhausted from the day
too tired to fall asleep.
Already looking forward
to go again next week.

Family

Gathered together
with loved ones from far and near
sharing a moment.

Births, picnics, birthdays,
holidays, showers, weddings
times to stay in touch.

Traditions bind us.
Passed down from those before us.
Mainstays through the years.

Teens on the Loose

Sisters whispered in secret
so no one could hear.
Their plans to run away
leaving their parents raw with fear.

Burdensome restrictions
motivated their desire.
Believed there was something better
on the other side to acquire.

Willing doors had opened
to welcome each of them in.
Keeping them out of the elements
and the streets where they had been.

Freedom lasted only a moment
before a greater force stepped in.
Their foolish act of rebellion
caused anguish to their parents and kin.

The sisters were driven back home.
Not a word was spoken between them.
Thoughts of what their parents would do
left them feeling pretty grim.

Grounded for what seemed an eternity
for the actions they believed were wise.
Learned a hard truth the day they left
that parents were not enemies, but allies.

They realized the time would one day come
when leaving home would be right.
Independence does not mean freedom.
It begins with maturity and insight.

The Intruder

At dawn,
the sound of shattered glass
hit the living room floor.
The noise from the crash
signaled danger entered the door.

The mother went to investigate.
Her daughters stayed behind.
Careful not to create
more worry on her mind.

A burly man was standing
in the center of the room.
His presence quite commanding
a feeling of impending doom.

He demanded her jewelry and money
as he threatened with words of harm.
He laughed as though it was funny
his aggression was meant to alarm.

With no money to offer
no valuables to render
desperation clung to mother
but she could not surrender.

Her daughters heard the message
and knew what had to be done.
They turned the tables of leverage
so it would be four against one.

With no time to waste
one daughter leapt from a window.
She got to her feet in haste
and ran to a nearby widow.

Two daughters ran to their room
pulled wooden slats from their beds
to strike the man who loomed
over their mother's head.

They stood hidden out of sight
and waited for the sound of sirens.
Afraid but prepared to fight
like cubs protecting mother lion.

Wailing in the far distance
the police sirens rang out.
Excited to know assistance
was on the way, no doubt.

The man tried to get away
when he realized his end was near.
The woman blocked his pathway
so the intruder could not disappear.

Several police officers arrived
the burly man was captured.
Glad everyone survived
and shouted in joyous rapture.

Relieved the ordeal was over
grateful to the kind officers.
Now there could be closure
for the daughters and their mother.

The violation awakened them
to a whole new reality.
A person's safety is like a gem
especially when it is family.

Part V
A Seed Sprouts

Its growth depends on the condition
of the soil and how much it's fed.

Who Will I Be?

Ask a young child
who they want to be.
Some will not know
Others will answer quickly.

Rarely does an answer
reflect what is inside.
Children dream mirror expectations
from others as their guide.

If given a chance to say
how they really feel
a child's first response
would be very real.

Their words are true
straight from the heart.
They say what they mean
right from the start.

When I looked back
to my girlhood years
I remembered this question
which prompted some fears.

It was hard to know
what I would be.
The path so uncertain
the choices so varied.

Maybe, the best response
for a child that is key,
is to say, "When I grow up,
I just want to be me."

Flower Girl

Little hands
scattered rose petals
along the grassy path.

Her innocence admired
by all who witnessed.

A child-like version
of the one being celebrated.

Going before the bride
like an angel
guiding her
down the path
to a new life.

She hoped
that one day
it will be her turn
to walk among the petals
into another's arms.

A Little Girl's Best Friend

The red leather diary
sat on the little girl's nightstand
next to her bed.

Her monogrammed initials
stamped on the front cover.
Trimmed with gold-edged pages.
Locked with a tiny key
that dangled from its latch.

Written inside
were the vivid imaginings
of the little girl's secret world.
Her words brought life
onto the pages of her diary.

When the girl was happy
she wrote about her family
friends and the things
she liked to do.
Sometimes she drew pictures
when she could not find
the right words.

She loved to write songs
and match the words
to the music from
her favorite song
or commercial jingle.

When she was sad
she wrote so hard
on the pages of her diary
that it scored straight through
to the other side.

One day,
a boy from school teased her
in front of her friends.
He was always teasing her.

She fought back
by writing a jingle
filled with angry words
and set them to the tune
of her favorite Motown song.

The next time he teased her
she sung the song to him
in front of his friends.

It was the last time
he bothered her.
Her words convince him
to pick on someone else.

Now,
all grown up
she does not write
in a diary anymore.

It is packed away
only to be opened
when she wants to remember
the girl she used to be.

On those days,
her old friend returns to life.
The pages bring laughter
also a few tears.

She remembers the days
when her words flowed freely
raw with emotion, uncorrupted
unhindered by time.

As she reads
her little red diary
hope fills her soul again.
Dreams come alive.
Excitement stirs within her.

She buys another
red leather diary
trimmed with gold-edged pages
containing a lock and key.

She writes out a plan
to realize her dreams
and revives herself once more.

Your Birth Day

The day that you were born
you were a treasure to behold.
Arrived in perfect timing
a miracle of old.

There is no one else like you.
Nor will there ever be.
Just like a snowflake or fingerprint
you are you, fully and free.

Everything you are
is portioned in the right amount,
even the hairs on your head
are something you cannot count.

The substance of your life
is recycled every day.
To form something fresh and new
to experience in a different way.

A new idea, a new choice
a new beginning with the dawn.
To dream, to visualize
to pursue what you thought was gone.

A Birthday Celebration

A shy girl
who had very few friends
would be celebrating
her seventh birthday.

Her parents decided
to give her a skating party.

They invited
relatives, classmates
and Sunday school friends.

Many people came
bringing gifts, food, and well wishes.

Skaters squeezed onto
the skating rink floor.
Young and old alike
bebopped to the music.

Later,
a chorus of voices
rang out with the

happy birthday song.
Sodas and birthday cake
were passed around.

In a rush to return
to the skating rink,
the delights were
tossed about, half-eaten.

The shy girl
was so happy.
She realized she had
more friends than
she knew.

A Thorn in Her Side

Outside with friends
playing a game of
hide-and-go seek.
She was struck by a
stabbing pain
that seared her right side.

A swelling
below the belly
made it clear that
a medical emergency
was on the rise.

Unable to walk
caught the attention
of a well-meaning neighbor.
She alerted the girl's mother
who called for help.

Appendicitis was the diagnosis.
The doctor said

there was a thorn in her side
like the ones
on the stems of roses
which needed to be removed.

After the operation,
the girl was pampered
by the hospital staff
like a diva child star.

On the day of her release
she did not want to leave.
Her secret wish
was to return to the hospital
with a thorn on the other side.

Sleep Snatcher

When I was very young
I would lie awake at night
determined to uncover
when darkness seized the light.

I tried to figure out
the instant this took place.
To find out what happens
in this sleep snatcher mystery case.

Curious to know
the boundary between the lines
when a person crosses over
from coherence to sublime.

The answer to the puzzle
has yet to be made known.
Once we fall asleep
to dream is enough alone.

Stolen Kisses

In the summer,
neighborhood children
stayed all day outdoors.

A favorite game
we used to play
was hide-and-go-seek.

We sought out
places to hide
not wanting
to be easily found.

Behind a tree
in a garage
tucked away
in a crawl space
underneath a house
behind a lattice fence.

The boy next door
hid with me.
When we faced each other
he would steal a kiss.

Each place we hid
offered another chance
for him to steal
one more kiss.

Too young
to know desire
nor feel the passion of
the moment.

A kiss was just a kiss.
In an instant,
the event quickly passed
and we ran off
to join the others
for another game.

Pen Pals

Letter writing
a favorite pastime.
Stationery chosen with care.
Embossed lettering
personalize each page.

The recipient of my
letters was a favorite aunt
whose husband was
in the military.

They traveled the world
and lived in faraway places.

Fascinated by the stamps
that marked each letter
inspired me to find out more.

But,
more important
was the time she took

to write her young niece
about the sights and experiences
she embraced.

Reading her letters
opened my young mind
to visions I might never see.
I cherished every word.

My French Teacher

French,
a language
sweet to the ears.
A flavorful sound
to the soul.

A culture of delights
old-world charm
leading trends in high fashion.
An inspiration to the world.

My seventh-grade French teacher
embodied the culture.
A classic beauty
fresh, simple, fashionable.

Pencil skirts
matching sweater sets
kitten-heeled pumps
tastefully worn.

A pixie-style hair cut
with bangs swept
across her forehead.

Nails cut short
painted with clear nail polish.
Shimmering lip gloss
moistened her lips.

A delicate silver chain
graced her neck
supporting a tiny cross
that dangled from the center.

The elegant image
who stood before the class
unknowingly offered
a glimpse of what was possible
for the young girls who observed.

Because young girls and boys
are always on the lookout
for significant others
to show them the way.

A Neighborhood Haven

Growing up,
the neighborhood library
was a place to escape
from the outside world.

Minutes melted away
in the depths
of a good book
or children's magazine.

A library card
was my passport
to the world.

Every book
opened possibilities
for adventure.

I learned about
how children lived
and the things they liked to do
in other countries.
I learned about fun
activities to do
when I was not reading.

I met new friends
through characters
in a chapter book or novel.

I listened to stories
read by the librarians.

My imaginations
came to life
in the quiet spaces
of the library.

So, it is no surprise
that when I grew up
I became a librarian.

Sleepovers

The teenage girls
in my family
occasionally planned
weekend sleepovers.

Equipped with
sleeping bags
finger foods
movies and games
ready for a weekend
of fun.

We sat in a circle
on the floor
talked about boys
funneled secrets and gossip
around the room.

Ears tingled to hear
the latest gossip.

After a while,
conversation waned
bored for something
else to do.

Suddenly,
the sounds of Motown
sliced through the room.
We jumped to our feet
moving to the beat.

Someone always
knew the latest
dance trends
featured on the
national television show
called "Soul Train."

New steps
choreographed to the music
taught by the cousin
who knew what dances
were echoed
across the country.

Each dance had a name
with its special moves.

Once learned,
we passed them on to others
outside our circle.
It was the best part
of our time together.
Because dancing
spoke a language
we all understood.

Hope Toward the Future

On my sixteenth birthday,
I was given a cedar-infused hope chest
carved with etched designs
scrolled across the front.
A cushioned leather seat
adorned the top.

By tradition,
the first-born daughter
in the family
received this gift
to be filled with lingerie,
household items, linens
and dishware needed
in anticipation for married life.

My chest was filled
with all the beautiful items
a young woman desired
as a new bride.

But also,
it was filled with
questions about my future.

As I stuffed my treasure box
with various pieces,
I wondered,
"Whom would I marry?"
"Would I be a good wife and mother?"
"How would I impact the world?"
"Would I be strong and courageous?"
"Would I stay true to myself?"

Now,
with many years behind me
my hope chest is no longer
filled with the items once needed
for a young bride.

It is filled with many treasures
not to be forgotten.
Letters, cards, and keepsakes
of family and friends.
Eulogies of people no longer here.

One day,
those treasures will be evidence
of my life and all I cherished
to be remembered by those I
leave behind.

Rebel with a Cause

An adolescent girl
in a woman's body
still a child
encumbered with
grown up responsibilities.

Torn between two worlds.
Too young to receive
the rites of passage.
Too old to hang on to child's play.

Resistance stretched out
in all she did
in all she felt.
She yearned to be free.

To break away
from the limitations
placed on her
because of age and tradition.

Smothered under the rules
of an old way.
She desired something different.

Impulsive for change.
Seeking excitement.
Overriding rationality.

She protested against
parental establishment
causing discord and indifference
against the ones who knew best.

Inclined to listen
to those considered peers
traveling down the same road
as she.

She could not perceive
the many lessons to learn
on the way to adulthood.

Patience and understanding
were displayed
by those more experienced.

They knew
she would continue
to change shape
like the caterpillar
to the butterfly.
Before long,
the time would come

when the cocoon
of childhood
would break open
and the adult emerged.

Who she became next
only time would determine.

The End of Childhood

Children reach the age
when it is time to leave home
to find their own way.

Unsure of their steps
encounter many pitfalls
along the broad path.

Trial and error
produce wisdom to change course
refining their stride.